Meet the
PITTSBURGH STEELERS

BY
ZACK BURGESS

NORWOOD HOUSE PRESS

CHICAGO, ILLINOIS

NORWOODHOUSE ◆ PRESS

P.O. Box 316598 • Chicago, Illinois 60631
For more information about Norwood House Press please visit our website at
www.norwoodhousepress.com or call 866-565-2900.

Photo Credits:
All photos courtesy of Associated Press, except for the following: Topps, Inc. (6, 10 both, 11 top),
Black Book Archives (7, 23), NFL Pro Line (11 middle), Fleer Corp. (11 bottom), Xerographics (18),
Pro Set (22).

Cover Photo: Frank Franklin II/Associated Press

The football memorabilia photographed for this book is part of the authors' collection. The collectibles used
for artistic background purposes in this series were manufactured by many different card companies—
including Bowman, Donruss, Fleer, Leaf, O-Pee-Chee, Pacific, Panini America, Philadelphia Chewing Gum,
Pinnacle, Pro Line, Pro Set, Score, Topps, and Upper Deck—as well as several food brands, including
Crane's, Hostess, Kellogg's, McDonald's and Post.

Designer: Ron Jaffe
Series Editors: Mike Kennedy and Mark Stewart
Project Management: Black Book Partners, LLC.
Editorial Production: Lisa Walsh

LIBRARY OF CONGRESS CATALOGING-IN-PUBLICATION DATA
Names: Burgess, Zack.
Title: Meet the Pittsburgh Steelers / by Zack Burgess.
Description: Chicago, Illinois : Norwood House Press, [2016] | Series: Big
    picture sports | Includes bibliographical references and index. |
    Audience: Grade: K to Grade 3.
Identifiers: LCCN 2015026319| ISBN 9781599537498 (Library Edition : alk.
    paper) | ISBN 9781603578523 (eBook)
Subjects: LCSH: Pittsburgh Steelers (Football team)--Miscellanea--Juvenile
    literature.
Classification: LCC GV956.P57 B87 2016 | DDC 796.332/640974886--dc23
LC record available at http://lccn.loc.gov/2015026319

288N—072016
Manufactured in the United States of America in North Mankato, Minnesota

CONTENTS

Words in **bold type** are defined on page 24.

The Steelers play with toughness and joy.

CALL ME A STEELER

Steel is used to build structures such as buildings and bridges. The Pittsburgh Steelers are named after the people who make steel. They are among the toughest workers in the world. Fans in Pittsburgh believe their Steelers are just as tough.

The Steelers played their first season in the National Football League (NFL) in 1933. Coach Chuck Noll guided them to four Super Bowl victories in the 1970s. They also won in 2006 and 2009. Two of their greatest leaders were **Terry Bradshaw** and Ben Roethlisberger.

Terry Bradshaw

Ben Roethlisberger spots an open teammate.

Fans have great views at the Steelers' stadium.

Best Seat in the House

Fans never miss a play in the Steelers' stadium. Every seat has a good view of the field. The stadium is located on Art Rooney Avenue. Rooney started the Steelers in 1933. His family still owns the team.

JOE KRU...
DEF. TACKLE   PITTSB...

SHOE BOX

The trading cards on these pages show some of the best Steelers ever.

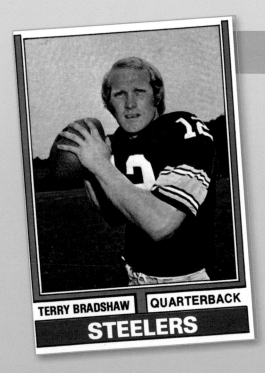

TERRY BRADSHAW | QUARTERBACK
STEELERS

TERRY BRADSHAW

QUARTERBACK · 1970-1983

Terry had a strong arm and a big heart. He loved throwing long passes for touchdowns.

FRANCO HARRIS

RUNNING BACK · 1972-1983

No one wanted to tackle Franco when he busted through the line. He ran for more than 1,000 yards eight times.

Franco Harris

JACK LAMBERT

LINEBACKER · 1974-1984

Jack put fear into running backs and receivers. He was the NFL's Defensive Player of the Year in 1976.

ROD WOODSON

CORNERBACK · 1987-1996

Rod was a sprinter in college. He had 38 **interceptions** for the Steelers.

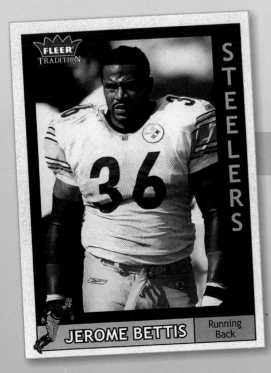

JEROME BETTIS

RUNNING BACK · 1996-2005

Jerome's nickname was "The Bus." He liked to run over tacklers, instead of around them!

THE BIG PICTURE

Look at the two photos on page 13. Both appear to be the same. But they are not. There are three differences. Can you spot them?

Answers on page 23.

13

True or False?

Ben Roethlisberger was a star quarterback. Two of these facts about him are **TRUE**. One is **FALSE**. Do you know which is which?

1 Ben threw the winning touchdown in the Steelers' 2009 Super Bowl victory.

2 Ben was the tallest quarterback in NFL history.

3 A restaurant in Pittsburgh named a sandwich after Ben called "The Roethlis Burger."

Answer on page 23.

Ben Roethlisberger celebrates a touchdown.

Steelers fans are always ready to wave the "Terrible Towel."

Go Steelers, Go!

Pittsburgh fans are some of the most loyal in the NFL. They are famous for waving their "Terrible Towels." The Steelers love seeing thousands of fans twirling their towels at once. It always gives them an extra boost of energy.

ON THE MAP

Here is a look at where five Steelers were born, along with a fun fact about each.

 1 **TROY POLAMALU · GARDEN GROVE, CALIFORNIA**
Troy was famous for his long hair and for making plays all over the field.

 2 **JOE GREENE · TEMPLE, TEXAS**
Joe was voted into the **Hall of Fame** in 1987.

 3 **MIKE WEBSTER · TOMAHAWK, WISCONSIN**
Mike was an **All-Pro** five times for the Steelers.

 4 **MEL BLOUNT · VIDALIA, GEORGIA**
Mel made the **Pro Bowl** five times for the Steelers.

 5 **ERNIE STAUTNER · CHAM, GERMANY**
Ernie was the team's top defensive star in the 1950s.

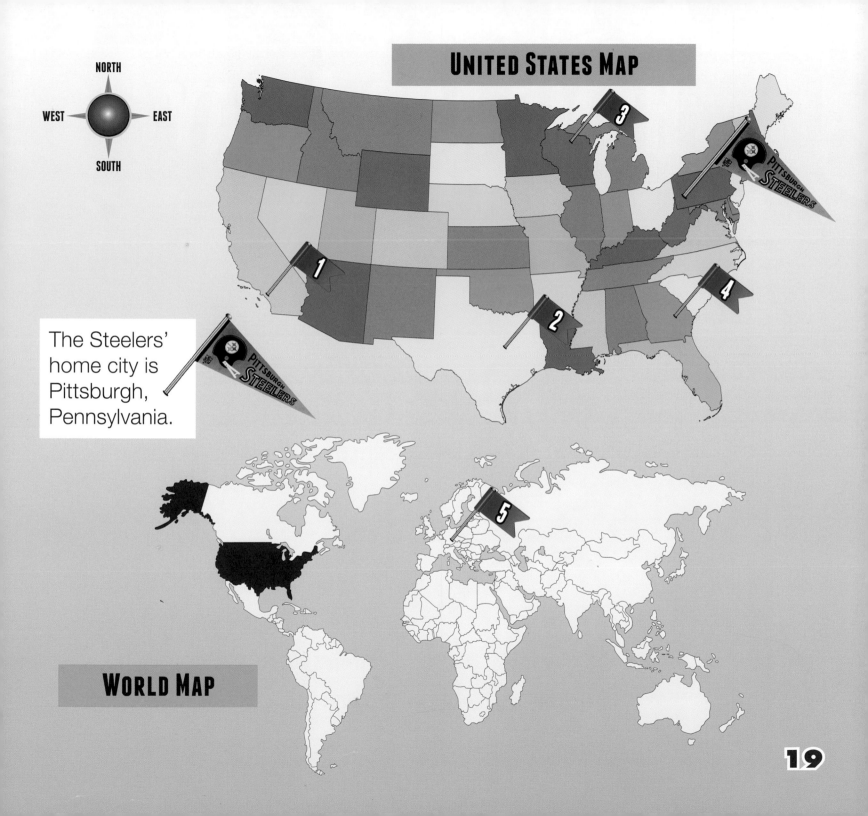

NORTH

WEST ● EAST

SOUTH

3

PITTSBURGH STEELERS

1

2

4

The Steelers' home city is Pittsburgh, Pennsylvania.

PITTSBURGH STEELERS

5

WORLD MAP

Le'Veon Bell wears the Steelers' home uniform.

Football teams wear different uniforms for home and away games. For more than 80 years, the Steelers' main colors have been black and yellow-gold. They added white in the 1960s.

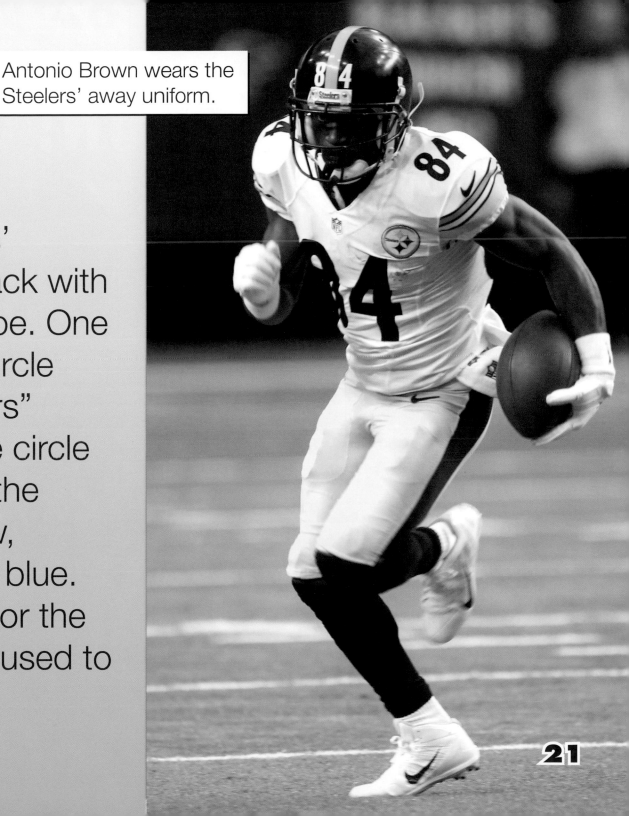

Antonio Brown wears the Steelers' away uniform.

The Steelers' helmet is black with a yellow stripe. One side has a circle with "Steelers" inside it. The circle also shows the colors yellow, orange, and blue. They stand for the three things used to make steel.

WE WON!

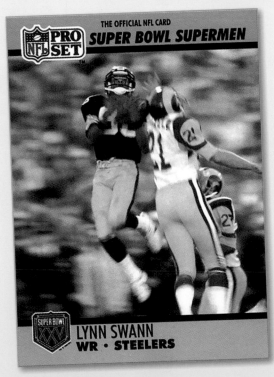

THE OFFICIAL NFL CARD
SUPER BOWL SUPERMEN

LYNN SWANN
WR · STEELERS

The Steelers and their fans expect an NFL championship every season. They have won the Super Bowl six times. Often, receivers made the winning plays. Hines Ward, Santonio Holmes, and **Lynn Swann** were each Most Valuable Player of the Super Bowl.

RECORD BOOK

These Steelers set team records.

PASSING YARDS	RECORD
Season: Ben Roethlisberger (2014)	4,952
Career: Ben Roethlisberger	42,995

RECEIVING YARDS	RECORD
Season: Antonio Brown (2015)	1,834
Career: **Hines Ward**	12,083

RUSHING YARDS	RECORD
Season: Barry Foster (1992)	1,690
Career: Franco Harris	11,950

ANSWERS FOR THE BIG PICTURE
#56 changed to #59, #34's towel disappeared, and the circle on #49's jersey changed to yellow.

ANSWER FOR TRUE AND FALSE
#2 is false. Ben was not the tallest quarterback in NFL history.

All-Pro
An honor given to the best NFL player at each position.

Hall of Fame
The museum in Canton, Ohio, where football's greatest players are honored.

Interceptions
Passes caught by a defensive player.

Pro Bowl
The NFL's annual all-star game.

Photos are on **BOLD** numbered pages.

ABOUT THE AUTHOR

Zack Burgess has been writing about sports for more than 20 years. He has lived all over the country and interviewed lots of All-Pro football players, including Brett Favre, Eddie George, Jerome Bettis, Shannon Sharpe, and Rich Gannon. Zack was the first African American beat writer to cover Major League Baseball when he worked for the *Kansas City Star*.

ABOUT THE STEELERS

Learn more at these websites:

www.steelers.com • www.profootballhof.com

www.teamspiritextras.com/Overtime/html/steelers.html